T0164676

HOW TO FIND YOUR INNER GLOW.

A Meditation with Babaji

GERI MCKELLAR

BALBOA.
PRESS

A DIVISION OF HAY HOUSE

Balboa Press books may be ordered through booksellers or by contacting:

Balboa Press
A Division of Hay House
1663 Liberty Drive
Bloomington, IN 47403
www.balboapress.com
1 (877) 407-4847

Because of the dynamic nature of the Internet, any web addresses or
links contained in this book may have changed since publication and
may no longer be valid. The views expressed in this work are solely those
of the author and do not necessarily reflect the views of the publisher,
and the publisher hereby disclaims any responsibility for them.

The author of this book does not dispense medical advice or prescribe the use
of any technique as a form of treatment for physical, emotional, or medical
problems without the advice of a physician, either directly or indirectly. The
intent of the author is only to offer information of a general nature to help
you in your quest for emotional and spiritual well-being. In the event you use
any of the information in this book for yourself, which is your constitutional
right, the author and the publisher assume no responsibility for your actions.

Any people depicted in stock imagery provided by Thinkstock are
models, and such images are being used for illustrative purposes only.
Certain stock imagery © Thinkstock.

Printed in the United States of America.

ISBN: 978-1-4525-8428-7 (sc)
ISBN: 978-1-4525-8429-4 (e)

Library of Congress Control Number: 2013918415

Balboa Press rev. date: 1/10/2014

How to Find Your Inner Glow.

A Meditation with Babaji

GERI MCKELLAR

BALBOA.
PRESS

A DIVISION OF HAY HOUSE

Balboa Press books may be ordered through booksellers or by contacting:

Balboa Press
A Division of Hay House
1663 Liberty Drive
Bloomington, IN 47403
www.balboapress.com
1 (877) 407-4847

Because of the dynamic nature of the Internet, any web addresses or
links contained in this book may have changed since publication and
may no longer be valid. The views expressed in this work are solely those
of the author and do not necessarily reflect the views of the publisher,
and the publisher hereby disclaims any responsibility for them.

The author of this book does not dispense medical advice or prescribe the use
of any technique as a form of treatment for physical, emotional, or medical
problems without the advice of a physician, either directly or indirectly. The
intent of the author is only to offer information of a general nature to help
you in your quest for emotional and spiritual well-being. In the event you use
any of the information in this book for yourself, which is your constitutional
right, the author and the publisher assume no responsibility for your actions.

Any people depicted in stock imagery provided by Thinkstock are
models, and such images are being used for illustrative purposes only.
Certain stock imagery © Thinkstock.

Printed in the United States of America.

ISBN: 978-1-4525-8428-7 (sc)
ISBN: 978-1-4525-8429-4 (e)

Library of Congress Control Number: 2013918415

Balboa Press rev. date: 1/10/2014

Contents

Foreword

I am privileged to have been asked by my dear friend, Geri, to write an introduction to *How to Find Your Inner Glow,* which has, for me, the quite unique appeal – amongst recent Western spiritual writings – of being based upon personal experience rather than theory. Whilst Geri has studied extensively with Buddhist teachers over the years, she is a natural medium and sensitive and I have personally witnessed many of her intuitions and insights. Geri's spiritual experiences have nudged her in the right direction time and time again in the search for truth, wisdom and inner peace and, ultimately, the search for God.

When Geri was given the challenge, in an out-of-body visitation from Babaji, of writing a book to encourage anyone – everyone – to try meditation as a quick and easy remedy for the trials and tribulations of modern life, I knew about it the next morning, and I knew she could do it, despite her misgivings. Babaji also had a very important message for Geri to deliver. For you, the reader, to start with it will be 'theory' but one that you can very easily prove by putting it straight into practice. It is a step-by-step guided meditation – a complete journey to a very special place of inner peace, helping us to find an inner smile and hopefully, in time, divine unity, as Geri has done – having used this method to help overcome a devastating illness – a form of meningitis – which completely wiped her out for eight months and continued to disable her for a further sixteen months, after which Babaji appeared and encouraged her to share what she had learned with you.

∞

Geri has used some terms and names within the text which may or may not be familiar to you, so I was asked to introduce the cast, as it were. Many of these are concepts which vary according to the source, so don't make faces at me if you've heard something different. Our minds are limited, but the Divine is not restricted to mind, so all things are possible; it is only humans who set limitations . . .

Shiva and Shakti: Generally thought of as the male and female principles; the first division of the One, the Source, the Undivided.

Shiva is usually represented as a young male sitting cross-legged, with the crescent moon in his hair, the Ganga river flowing over his head, and a bevy of cobras entwined around him. The Shakti may be represented as a young female of varied character and mood from the mildest, gentle Parvati to the scariest Kali, whom Geri talks to you about in this book. Both Shiva and Shakti may be experienced in these forms by those who are devoted to them, but they are actually states of consciousness – Shiva the motionless 'male' principle, Shakti the ever-active 'female'. Shiva and Shakti are widely thought of as husband and wife, as this is a simple way for the human mind to understand the more complex idea of complete union on a divine level.

In Hindu tradition, Shiva is also widely perceived as the third deity of the Hindu Trinity; Brahma the creator aspect, Vishnu the maintainer and Shiva the destroyer/regenerator.

'Baba' and 'Ji' are common terms in India – Baba being 'Father' and Ji 'Dear'. So, in spiritual circles, there is a lot of confusion as to which Baba or Babaji one is referring to. The Babaji whom Geri talks about is Haidakhan Babaji, thought of by his devotees as 'Avatar'. Avatar means direct incarnation or manifestation of God/The One. He is also widely thought to be a recent reincarnation of Hairakhan Babaji, a nineteenth-century saint from the same area in the Indian foothills of the Himalaya.

'Swami', strictly speaking, refers to a wandering renunciant, of which there are several orders in India. However, it is widely used as a term of respect and/or affection for a holy person. The Swami referred to is Sathya Sai Baba, who is also looked upon as Avatar by his devotees.

Meditation: The classical aim of meditation is to reunite the individual consciousness with the absolute consciousness – losing one's self in God. Other schools of thought use meditation for other ends, such as the relief of suffering. One has to allow the mind to become still in order to fully identify and unite with the divine.

∞

But now, why is this book for you? What, in short, will it do for you?

Well, perhaps you find yourself with a personality or a way of life which is difficult to cope with. Perhaps you get too involved in things, get overwhelmed and become hurt – and then feel there is nobody to turn to, no 'someone else' to explain your predicament to or help you find the answers. Perhaps, instead of enjoying the game of life you find yourself on the outside looking in – and feeling lost.

Or you may have realised, as many people do, that everything in the world isn't quite as real or straightforward as you once thought and now you want to know more. Questions may be buzzing around in your head about what you believe – and believe in – in this complex world of ours.

Alternatively you may be a young person starting out on life's journey, lacking self-confidence, perhaps through peer-pressure or other people's expectations and finding it hard to cope.

You may already be blessed with a happy disposition and long for others – your family and friends – to learn to be happy too.

And, of course, many people turn to meditation to help relieve very real personal suffering, whether physical or psychological. Hopefully, it will bring, at least, a moment of calm in the chaos of a busy mind. Whatever your objective Geri has brought some very ancient teachings together in a simple manner to help create space and peace in your mind, an inner glow, an inner smile and – in time – divine unity.

I must not conclude this introduction without telling you at least something about Geri McKellar. Geri is a gentle and modest person who hates to be in the spotlight. Suffice for me to say here that Geri has studied spiritual philosophy for over twenty-five years absorbing the teachings and experience of some of the great masters, following which a major realisation came as the result of the terrible illness from which she nearly died.

Luckily for us, she made a full recovery and is now, at 46, a shining example of how mind can win over matter. She has written this little gem to help you find peace and happiness – to find your inner glow – just as she has done.

Enjoy!

Graham

Acknowledgments

Thank you Babaji and Kali for giving me the confidence to actually put pen to paper. Thank you to all the teachers I have listened to over the years for passing on their wisdom.

Thank you to my dear friend, Graham Cailes, for going through what we have come to know fondly as 'the manuscript' with a fine-toothed comb, correcting my slips, and for our hours of friendly debate about the different traditions. Graham is a life-long student of the scriptures of many belief systems, a practitioner of hatha, kriya, jnana, dhyana, karma and bhakti yoga and, over the past few years, has tutored a small group in Sanskrit chant. Thank you to my special friend, Sonia Dear, for reading through with her questioning, objective mind. Thank you so much for your patience, guys!

Thank you also to my dear friends, who kindly read through the book for me, offering help and advice; you know who you are.

Thank you to my husband, renowned healer Andrew McKellar; my daughter, Kristie-Anne, who is featured on the front cover; and my son, Marcus, for his technical support. Thank you for letting me spend so much time in meditation and on retreats.

Thank you Bryan Halsey for your fine-tuning ready for publication.

Thank you to my niece, Lucy Randall, for the artwork on the front cover; to Ellie Breton for taking my author photographs with my dogs; and to Toni Jaman-Singh Waelti for his kindness in allowing me to use the beautiful photographs of Babaji.

I love you all!

Babaji Told Me to Write

January 2013: I have been mentally apologizing to Babaji for not writing, since he asked me to do so nearly two years ago, but this evening I have, at last, had inspiration and the realization of what Babaji actually wanted me to write.

∞

I have often had out-of-body experiences and, more than once, Babaji has visited me whilst I was out of my body . . .

March 2011: *I sat up in my bed and looked at the clock – 4:10 a.m. As I looked, I could see the clock clearly, but I could also see my physical body still asleep in my bed. My astral body had sat up, as I had been awakened by Babaji. He was lying on my bed, beaming at me, his skin beautiful, his hair dark and slightly dreadlocked; he looked very young and vibrant. He was wearing a traditional form of Indian dress called a dhoti. Lying on his stomach, chin in his hands, he smiled pure Divine Love at me.*

"Babaji, you are here again!" I exclaimed.

He tilted his head to one side and, with the sweetest smile, said, "Teach me."

"I can't teach you, Babaji; you know everything!" I protested.

"Yes, you can. Try!" he encouraged.

"Like what, Babaji?" I asked.

In that instant, by thought alone, Babaji conveyed to me all that I had learned from different teachers over the past twenty-five years, *but his mouth said:*

"About the violet flame and the quantum field."

"I can't teach you that, Babaji. You know everything, anyway," I replied, embarrassed at the fact that he would even ask me.

"Keep it simple." He laughed.

∞

Then, like magic, Babaji had a pen in his hand and he threw it at me. It spun over and over like a cartwheel. Although I was in my astral body, it still seemed to make a physical thud as it hit me and he said "Write!"

Then Babaji looked really sad. His face started to turn old and wrinkled and became that of Sai Baba. A tear ran down his cheek, and he said, "Baba has to go." His expression had such compassion and love, as if it were for every living being on the planet. I knew intuitively that he meant that a guru who was very precious to me was going to die, as I will explain later.

I started to cry. "Please don't go."

Then Babaji stood up – once more looking young and vibrant – walked around the end of my bed, said "Kali is on her way!" and vanished.

∞

I awoke with a jolt, looked at the clock, and sat up in my waking physical body. The time was 4:37 a.m. I just sat on the edge of my bed and sobbed. I knew I wouldn't see Babaji again until I had written what I had learned; I also felt I would never be able to do as he asked. I do not consider myself to be a writer, let alone an author. I am not very good at English and I am certainly no guru. I resigned myself to the fact that I would probably not have another visit from Babaji and, to cap it all, a great teacher whom I knew as 'Swami', was going to die.

It's been almost two years since that auspicious night and I have hardly been able to look at his picture since, as all I see is him throwing the pen at me and saying "Write!"

"I don't know where to start or what to write, Babaji," I say internally. "What could I possibly write that hasn't been written before in a much more professional and articulate way?"

Then my heart aches, because I know he won't be back until I do. I see his beautiful eyes and hair so clearly from that visitation, as if it were still happening.

19th January 2013 – I was sitting in my Gompa (a Buddhist term for a meditation room) when I had a strong sense of Babaji's presence and a powerful feeling that I might start writing a book there and then. That very night, at 1:00 a.m., I felt wide-awake and was literally buzzing with energy. Violet light filled the room, and when violet light fills my room I know I am about to encounter a spiritual insight. I grabbed pen and paper and didn't stop writing until 4:00 a.m. That happened four nights in a row and then, periodically, over the space of two to three weeks.

I have studied Buddhist teachings extensively over the years. I have read, heard, felt and received, in one way or another, a vast amount of wisdom from the most beautiful teachers (not all of them Buddhist) on my travels in England, India and Bali. I have covered the entire Buddhist path to Enlightenment and have been very fortunate to receive clear instruction on both the Compassion teachings and the Emptiness teachings, even the tantric paths, which my Buddhist teachers taught as a visualization technique whereby you fully identify with a chosen deity.

∞

It was at this point, when I had completed my studies and used the teachings to begin my recovery from a very serious illness, that I personally experienced the Buddhist teaching that all is 'Emptiness' – a kind of void, although one is taught it is most definitely not a void. It is endlessly compassionate but, seemingly, very impersonal. During my illness I had visions of the Divine Mother in the aspect of Mother Mary. This made me question a lot, because she wasn't 'Buddhist'. Since the beginning of my Buddhist training, I have had great faith in the deity Prajnaparamita, the Mother of all Buddhas. I had beautiful dreams of her. Then she transformed into Mother Mary and eventually Kali. A beautiful teacher said to me once, "Same God, different dress. All One." All One . . .

I had already meditated on this a lot when Babaji first appeared to me in my dream state, telling me not to worry, that he would get me back to my mother. At the time I didn't even know who Babaji was or why I needed to get back to my mother, although now it is perfectly clear, as I will explain – it symbolized reuniting with the Divine Mother aspect of God.

So I will attempt to share with you what Babaji conveyed to me that auspicious evening when he told me to teach him and to write – although I have the sneaking suspicion that the violet light that appears in my room also has a lot to do with what is written here – divine inspiration, if you will.

It's All Blue Sky

I feel as if I am writing this book backwards, because my present, truly deep realization has come full circle to the very first teaching I ever heard. The first teaching is the last teaching, but you just don't realize it until you have heard it many times. It's quite the cosmic joke once you get it! I had heard hundreds of teachings by many fully qualified spiritual guides before I really got it; you need to hear them over and over and, each time, the realization etches into your mind a bit deeper until someone says the same thing in a slightly different way and you think *'Ah, yes . . . light-bulb moment!'*

I hope this book may cut to the chase and bring the end result to the beginning. May Babaji bless every word of this little book and every mind that reads it. By the blessings of the Buddha, Shiva, the Divine Mother and all the holy beings, may you attain a bright 'Blue Sky' for your mind, an abode of peace, a lot quicker than I! To gain truly deep meaning, please try to read each sentence with deep thought and in a contemplative manner. The deeper you look, the deeper the meaning you will find. The first teaching I heard – at that stage only superficially – was that the mind is like a clear, blue sky and the thoughts like bad weather.

A Wish to Be Happy

Every single person's heart and mind is different. As I will explain, the heart and mind should act as one. If we were to reveal our minds to a holy being such as Babaji or a Buddha (Buddha means one who has awoken, one who is enlightened) we would probably feel a bit embarrassed at what they would see – quite possibly a murky mess of misery, pain, self-pity and desire. That's for starters. An enlightened one would have no judgement on this, just compassion for the pain we hold in our minds, which so often reflects in our physical bodies.

∞

How wonderful would it be if we could display our minds in an offering bowl to Babaji or a Buddha and it shone like a crystal-clear pool, still and serene? It really is not that difficult or such a far-off, distant, fantasy that we could actually have clarity and peace in our hearts and minds. This clarity helps us to heal our physical form and create love and peace around ourselves and others.

∞

The journey starts with a wish; a wish for inner peace and stillness — a wish to be happy and for those around us to be happy, too. It's all a reflection and perception. We need the wish to change our perception.

∞

For example, if we perceive someone as a rival or foe, *we* have formed an impression of that person and turned him or her into an 'enemy'. Our own angry minds have decided to view that person with contempt and judgment. Our anger has made our minds fearful, sad, and very restless. If we have uncomfortable minds, we have heavy hearts. This feeling makes us want to avoid the person who made us angry. Maybe there is nobody in your life who you view quite as strongly as this, but perhaps there is someone who, shall we say, causes you difficulty…'Enemy'.

When we perceive a stranger, often there is a feeling of indifference toward him or her, not really a strong emotion either way. This person may be nice or nasty. It doesn't really matter; it's neither here nor there – a kind of neutral feeling…'Stranger'.

Perceiving loved ones normally gives us feelings of joy and unity. There may be a sense of attachment or desire. Our minds project onto that loved one labels such as 'Lover,' 'Mother,' 'Father,' 'Sister', 'Friend'. *We* project the relationships we believe we should have with those individuals. We then expect them to behave in the way we feel appropriate. "Do as I say, and we will get along just fine." We expect them to act in ways we feel a relative, lover or friend should act… 'Loved One'.

∞∞∞

But expectations can soon end in disappointment when a relative, lover or friend acts in a way that displeases us or does not fulfil our expectations. This person could easily end up as a projected 'Rival' or 'Enemy', and we end up wishing to stay away from him or her. We need to aim for a balanced mind of unconditional love for friend or foe. It is a traditional Buddhist contemplation to find equally loving feelings for enemies, strangers, and loved ones.

Instead of blaming the other person for our problems we can start to develop the altruistic mind of unselfish concern for others by contemplating "How can I help you?"

A mother's love for her child is generally much less conditional than that in other relationships; often she only challenges her child if he or she is in danger, such as when the child is about to touch something hot and burn himself or herself or run into a road. She may then raise her voice, but only out of loving compassion and protection; otherwise she may watch with unconditional love as her child runs wild and free.

But even a mother's love can be conditional. She may wish, for instance, for her daughter to become a nurse and is bitterly disappointed and even angry when her daughter does not meet her expectations. If her child had gone along with her daydream, she could have been so proud and inflated her own ego; here the love of a mother is mixed with her own self-interest. Unconditional love does seem unrealistic but can be achieved.

Our minds easily oscillate from high expectations to thorough disappointment – up and down like a yoyo – with highs and lows. Happy one moment, angry the next, our minds change easily like the wind. We could laugh and joke one moment and then be upset and cry in an instant, especially when the joke is on us. The mind can so very easily be swayed, moved from a slight 'tut' to full-blown anger instantly.

Many of us can churn over all day something that made us tut in the morning. Perhaps a partner went to work without putting the bin out; after dwelling on it all day, it now becomes the reason for a major argument when he or she comes home. Dwelling on the irritation becomes the meditation for the day; thus, the person develops an angry state of mind. This causes separation, pushing relationships apart. Reunite with a peaceful heart. Problem solving is much easier when you come from a place of peace and love rather than a place of anger. 'Love'

∞∞∞

STOP!

We just need to stop. Stop the mind in its tracks. *Stop!* Just stop the mind running away with the

thought that caused that angry, state of mind that, in turn, caused a heavy heart. Uneasy, anxious feelings are even caused by what we think is love. What we feel to be love causes pain; 'love hurts', as the expression goes.

If we are 'in love' and it is one-sided, it causes feelings such as wanting, craving, grasping and yearning, any of which lead to an anxious mind and heavy heart. Even if it is mutual, but tainted by expectations, it causes pain. This pain causes us to blame the other when our desires are not met and things do not go our way. Others cannot make us happy. Happiness truly is within.

We need to learn to simply take the mind off the cause of pain and place it on a cause of peace. Stop dwelling on past hurts and future conquests. We need a pleasantly restful space to place the mind.

Finding that space is not difficult if we put in some basic training; as with anything, the more effort we put in, the more we get out. With some effort in training the mind, we can find a very comfortable space where there is both relief and peace. With effort, we can attain real, peaceful results and eventually happily accept almost any situation.

The training is easy; the more space you find the more you will seek, because, in those moments of clear space, you glimpse a feeling of peace. That peace expands and flows over into your day, your world and those of everyone in it. It is life-transforming. The first glimpse of that tranquil space entices you to search ever more deeply.

Training Begins

To begin the training, first start *watching* the mind.

Become the observer. We can learn to see the mind in two parts; although there are actually many aspects to the mind, for this purpose, we need to be aware of the conscious mind and the unconscious mind. The conscious mind is the part used, with full awareness, to think when one needs to do so. The unconscious mind is the entity that produces all sorts of random thoughts whenever *you are not consciously thinking*. It simply hates not to be doing something.

Above both of these is the Witness – the Atma or Divine Essence. The mind constantly chatters; for instance, it will keep going over the argument of that morning, even when you are trying to get to sleep that night. In fact, it seems as if the mind gets worse, even busier, whenever you are trying to get to sleep. It is just more noticeable at night, because that's when it disturbs us and we want it to stop! Even whilst sleeping, the mind is busy dreaming or, perhaps, having nightmare experience; the mind is never naturally quiet.

Become aware of the noisy running commentary in the mind, and then become aware of the part of the mind that can actually objectively listen to the constant dialogue. Find the part of the mind that is aware of that song that keeps going around and around in your head and wants to stop it. We can call this the silent witness. *Silently watching the chatterbox mind.* This part of the mind points out the chatter allowing us to calm, or even stop, it.

∞

A part of the conscious mind – that can be used to watch the stream of unconscious thoughts – can be imagined to be like a little fish that swims, just below the surface of the pond, without disturbing the water. The little fish can be thought of as one's alertness. The mind can be likened to a vast ocean that should be still and serene, but waves of thought create great disturbance.

The chatterbox mind causes waves; the little fish of alertness reminds us to be still and stop chattering, and then it can just watch the stillness within the ocean of the heart and mind. Use the mind to control the mind. Eventually, even the little fish dissolves . . . Gurus of all traditions, across the ages, have encouraged and inspired their students to watch the mind for thoughts, positive or negative, that disturb meditation and everyday life.

∞

This is the start of true meditation; watching the mind. Watching mainly for any disturbing thoughts; one could say thoughts that are more judgemental than those of a mother's unconditional love. The moment the mind tuts it has switched into angry mode; this is the perfect time to stop and switch it to the peaceful space of patience.

Patience is the antidote to anger and it is the beginning of true love and compassion. Patience is a key to the beautiful mind we need to develop. An irritated mind will propel us out of meditation and disturb our peace. If the doorbell goes whilst we are in meditation and we become annoyed, we have missed the point! Patience will keep us calm. We must not supress our anger or pretend it is not there, but truly and honestly feel no upset – from the heart. Changing the mind from 'Poor me' to 'How can I help you?' is the key to this.

∞

If we see someone acting out of anger, envy or jealousy, it is because he or she is suffering some sort of internal anguish in the mind and heart;

because he or she is hurting. Most people only get angry because they do not get their own way. Even if we get angry in the process of protecting a loved one, it is because we do not want them to be harmed or insulted. We want them to be safe and happy.

Think of any time *you* have been angry; it was, usually, because you didn't get your own way or felt defensive. You can still defend a loved one in a patient manner. Not getting what one wants can cause so much depression that one may feel life is not worth living. Finding space and clarity in the mind can really help to turn this around. A peaceful space *is there* to be found! Instead of acting out of anger, we can deal with angry, jealous people with reason and in a peaceful way. This would be much more helpful to both ourselves and others.

A wish that every living being could be happy and free from mental pain and heartache is a powerful step on the path to Enlightenment but, until we can understand and change our own minds, how can we truly help others?

∞

Calm, patient Loving Kindness

So, if we can view a bad-tempered person as a person in turmoil, we can view him or her with compassion and find patience in our hearts. With patience comes a kind of stillness with which we can defuse difficult, angry situations. With an even temper and perseverance, we can develop patience. Nobody wants to be unhappy; we can surely empathize with this. Empathy encourages us onward to help others in their pursuit for happiness. Mastering patience is the dawning of equanimity.

Obviously, in extreme cases of anger where there is danger, you should just remove yourself from the situation. In everyday angry situations, patience and loving kindness towards the one suffering the mental anguish of anger, is the way to your own inner peace – and that of others around you. *It's no good fighting fire with fire; it only causes an inferno.* Calm, loving patience is capable of extinguishing the fire.

In everyday life, to start training the mind for meditation, nip it – the mind – in the bud! Stop dwelling on noisy, uncomfortable tutting minds. Take the mind off what is annoying you and put it onto patient, compassionate stillness. Stop dwelling and start *Being.*

Stop dwelling on what made you tut – what caused the irritation – and exchange that mind for a mind of patience. It is easy if you *really* want to find inner peace. *Just do it!*

We can do this by changing our perceptions of an angry person to that of a poor, suffering, sad person. This will create a wish to help the person, rather than to avoid him or her. We will not be so affected by the person's *perceived* nastiness. If we are insulted and we have become familiar with a mind of patience, in time it will be like the person throwing stones through a clear, blue sky. The words will just flow through and out the other side. I use the term 'Blue Sky' to help visualize that concept.

Abusive words only have power to hurt if caught in a cloudy mind. When one can master the art of patience, words, thoughts and feelings will be like clouds dispersing in that clear, Blue Sky. Using patience to overcome anger is a traditional Buddhist method and is very basic Dharma also used by pre-Buddhist Indian traditions. Simplicity!

∞

So, the little fish is on guard, to watch silently and to help to remind us when to stop dwelling on irritations and start 'Being'. It reminds us to be patient, creating stillness and space, calming the ocean of thoughts. We can liken the busy heart and mind to a rough ocean of turmoil. With practice, we can calm the heart and mind to reveal a vast 'Ocean of Stillness'. The ocean dissolves into a clear, Blue Sky.

Happiness is a state of mind. It cannot be found in physical things. Love may be great in the honeymoon period, but a new partner will definitely bring a new set of irritations! Thinking that a new job will make you happy and solve all your problems, is a mistake unless you accept that there will be new issues to overcome. Some of us may yearn for a larger garden but, in reality, this will only create more gardening – and more weeds!

Anything – any *thing* – brings happiness only until we are no longer satisfied with the new acquisition, or the problems outweigh the perceived benefits. A thing only brings temporary, not lasting, happiness. This realization can help us to accept that there will always be problems, so why should we be surprised? Why get angry? It will not solve the problem but only make it worse.

∞

Contentment is one of the most powerful states of mind in allowing us to be truly happy and is very much worth practicing. Being content in every situation doesn't mean we shouldn't strive for success and gain but be content and patient with the actual journey towards our goals and with the end result, whatever it may be.

The path towards our goals shouldn't involve anger and bitterness, a dog-eat-dog mentality, or stepping on anyone who gets in the way. The alternative is to patiently, and with inner contentment, accept that this is where 'I Am' at this moment, moving steadfastly and peacefully along the path toward attaining the goal. Be content. Wise men and women across the ages have always taught this.

∞

Being still in the moment is the most powerful place in the entire Universe – the Cosmos even!

Where *is* the moment? It is when we stop the chattering mind for a moment – and to stop the chattering mind takes a great deal of effort, patience and contentment. Be content to patiently sit and quieten the mind and then, with effort, *stop* the chatter.

We need to stop the mind from dwelling on the past and planning the future, for the past has ceased to exist and the future has not yet arrived. It is in the moment that there is no mind, no me, no *I*.

When we can truly find the razor-edged balance of *this* moment, we become lost and found all at the same time. We become one with everything.

There is no separation and no obstruction; one's true nature revealed. It's all Blue Sky . . .

∞

At what moment does the bulb become the shoot? At what moment does the shoot become the stem? At what moment does the bud become the flower? At what moment does the flower cease to exist? We can see from speeded-up film that, on an atomic level, the constant, ever-changing movement of the flower is steadfastly marching towards the moment of death until the regrowth and life bursts forth once more. It is the same for us humans – birth, ageing, sickness and death. *Perpetual rebirth, ageing, sickness, and death.*

We can see that all physical matter, such as the earth herself, is like an ocean of atomic soup, constantly changing. There is vast space inside atomic particles until even the tiniest particle is found to be – well, *space* – or rather, as quantum physics has confirmed, an ocean of energy, known as the field, in which things only take form when they are looked at. In the ever-changing, there is common space between the vibrating particles that buzz in and out of existence. We are searching for this space. Impermanence is the teaching of old that begins to lift the veil of illusion. It is the gateway to finding the eternal space – changing, changing, changing!

∞

The *never-changing,* constant, timeless space that is eternal is where the moment is. Atoms change; the space does not. 'I AM' – the space that everything moves within.

Our minds can access this space as eternal stillness, a source of eternal happiness and peace. We can find deep inner peace when we can learn to stop our chattering minds, our 'poor me' feelings and judgements and fully enter the timeless, eternal space of the moment.

Just as our bodies are not fixed and solid, but constantly changing and decaying, neither are our minds. We like to think of a solid 'me' or 'self' with its own opinions – how proud we are of our particular views of life. We feel our own views are the correct ones. Yet every single heart and mind on the planet has a different view of reality. No two minds are the same; yet we all feel we are right. Egos clash every passing minute of the day.

With this in mind have you considered that it might be wise, on occasion, to just agree and go along with the other person's opinion – let him or her win? Why not? Happily accept their point of view on the basis that they truly believe they are correct in their thinking. It may bring about peace.

Of course, we need wisdom; if another person's point of view will bring real danger or harm, the wise thing would be to disagree. However, even this can be done in a spirit of love; the other person may not have all the facts or experience to form a balanced view. Might we be able to help him or her? Or do *we* need to reappraise our own views? . . .

∞

Mind is made up of these opinions, thoughts and feelings. We can change our minds like the wind, proving that our thoughts are not fixed and solid. Rigid views can loosen with reason. Angry feelings can vanish with a smile. With training, we can stop the ego chatter, let our thoughts blow away and disperse on the wind and start to reveal the Blue Sky.

The nature of mind is vast, eternal clarity, full of space. Everything – our physical bodies, even bricks and mortar – are space-like. As I said earlier with respect to atoms, we too are composed of space and light, not solid.

∞

Another way to help us feel – and find – this space is by using a traditional Buddhist method of reasoning; to visualize peeling off layers of skin. You can imagine peeling a fruit until there is nothing left or, taking it a stage further, you could look closely at your own hand. If you were to visualize peeling the skin off your hand, putting it in a heap on the floor and then searching closely in that heap for skin, you would only find millions of skin cells. Under a high-powered microscope these would become tiny, separate particles, not touching and eventually space-like in nature. If you then took the veins and muscles out of your hand, put them onto the heap and searched closely, you would, again, not find a hand but red and white blood cells and a fleshy mess. Under a high-powered microscope, you would find the same space-like appearance. Take away the bones, dismantle the skeleton into a heap on the floor; you could grind the bones into a powder that would eventually blow away like dust on the wind. In place of your hand at the end of your wrist, you would only find empty space.

All physical phenomena are like this. I once saw a poor badger that had been killed on the road. It was blown up to twice its natural size as it lay dead at the edge of the road. I took the same route every day on the school run and, each day, the badger had decayed a little more, getting flatter and smaller until after a week or so, there was just a bit of hair stuck to the road – almost empty space where the poor badger had dissolved into emptiness. Obviously, other animals and birds had eaten parts, and car wheels had flattened it. But at the end of the day, there is a real, deep teaching in the life and death of that dear badger. Where did it go? It had vanished into empty space.

What we are aiming for is to allow ourselves to experience the feeling of infinite space within *everything* – no boundaries, no limits. That space is not space as we have been taught at school but a space filled with infinite Being, infinite Consciousness, infinite Bliss and infinite love – the One. Home in on those words *allow* and *feeling*. We can't make it happen; we just have to allow ourselves to experience it. There is nowhere to go, no path to travel. We must just allow ourselves to remember what we truly are; Truth itself!

The essence of the mind is vast, eternal clarity that appears as a clear, Blue Sky – merely perceiving. Within this, we create a fictional 'I'. 'I' am made up of past experiences, the baby, the toddler, the teenager, the middle-aged person, all of whom have gone; my thoughts, feelings and opinions all changing, moment by moment. 'I' am the ego clinging to my strong opinion. If we loosen our grasping at our past identities and strong opinions, we find space and realize that there is nothing that is a solid 'I' or 'me', just a collection of thoughts and feelings from past experiences that have all ceased to exist!

What we should look for in everything is empty space. When training the mind, after watching it during our daily lives for instances of chatter and judgement, there comes a point when we need to stop, sit still and meditate to truly experience the space-like peace.

Eventually, one will feel peace even whilst on the go. The following meditation will increase familiarity with the loving space, creating an abode of peace that can be found in an instant. We are in a human form and get easily upset. Meditation creates a place of refuge in the heart and mind so that we can be human whilst having a divine experience.

Clear. Boundless. Blue Sky

A Meditation

For this meditation, you will need to be as comfortable as possible. Choose somewhere you will not be disturbed. A meditation can take anything from five minutes to five hours – or much longer but, for this meditation, half an hour with no disturbance would be a great place to start. So, make a start when, in your heart, you know you have time to yourself – when you will not need to rush off anywhere. Allow yourself a solid half hour of searching for inner peace. It can be done; it's not impossible.

I suggest that you read this short meditation book two or three times to become familiar with the concept of this meditation before you start the clear half an hour. Sit in a comfortable chair with a cushion behind you, as it is extremely important to have your spine straight and supported. Place your feet flat on the floor, with eyes gently closed and hands resting in your lap. Place your right hand in your left hand, palms facing upward, thumbs touching.

As we practice training the mind, it is very important not to get sleepy, but to keep the mind alert and awake. Although the *body* will be relaxed, the mind needs to be alert.

Start by relaxing the body and finding the natural rhythm of the breath. You will naturally breathe even whilst sleeping, so you do not need to worry about how to breathe for this meditation; that would be a distraction in itself. Just breathe in through the nostrils and out through the nose and mouth, with the natural rhythm of your breath. Do not force deep breaths. Gently relax your breathing until you are comfortable. Use the breath as a cushion to rest the mind on.

Every word of this book so far is the meditation. Meditation has two stages. The first stage is contemplation – contemplating the meaning of the words *until they bring about a feeling* of what the words are trying to convey. Words can only lead you to the feeling. Once you have found it, you then hold it until it grows and becomes familiar to you. Eventually, that special feeling never leaves or you can, at least, pick it back up at a moment's notice. This is the second stage of the meditation – *holding the mind still and placing it on the special feeling.*

The feeling you are aiming for in this meditation is warm, glowing space in the heart and mind. Feel this warm, glowing space of a vast, clear, blue sky on a sunny afternoon expanding and growing at your heart. Remember how you have felt on a carefree day full of blue skies and inner smiles. Bring this feeling into your heart and mind. You are searching for space in the heart and mind, allowing all thoughts and feelings – even the body itself – to dissolve into empty sky like space.

Sitting comfortably, with no anticipation of moving for half an hour and no expectation of an end result (expectation and anticipation are not part of the moment; they will propel you out of meditation and into the future), bring the mind back to the comfortable chair. Become aware of your body relaxing as you settle into being here and now, remembering that you are searching for space; space within the atoms and space between the thoughts. Please be patient with the step-by-step instructions. They are all part of the training.

Mind, by nature, can be likened to a clear, Blue Sky and all our thoughts and feelings are like the clouds. Sometimes there is very stormy, angry weather in our minds; on other days, white, fluffy clouds that are easily dispersed by the sunshine, depending on our moods. Eventually, there will be no clouds – only spiritual sunshine, rays of unconditional love of the Divine Mother. It's not impossible.

Imagine now, if you will, an endless expanse of beautiful, bright, Blue Sky and rays of spiritual sunlight shining down onto your face. The rays are the perfect temperature – gentle, warm, healing rays making your face radiant in the light. Gently breathe in the light and breathe out any tension and stress. Breathe light in through the nostrils down into the lungs; see the light swirling around the lungs and back out through the nose and mouth. With every in-breath draw in the light and with every out-breath see tension and stress dissolve into light. Breathe in spiritual sunshine and breathe out spiritual sunshine. (Try to follow the instructions slowly and carefully with real concentration, even if you feel you have heard them all before.)

See the light filling your lungs, chest and heart with a beautiful, warm glow. Keep the rhythm of the breath natural; as the light enters the nostrils, every atom and cell becomes alive with light. See your nose and face light up; feel your eyes shining bright with light, brighter with every out-breath. Relax your jaw and facial muscles, as the jaw holds so much tension. The spiritual sunlight melts it all away, also melting the lines away from your forehead. See even the inside of your mouth, tongue and tonsils become alive with light, brighter with every out-breath.

Take time to really feel the light radiating around the inside of your brain and skull, even your ears. Be thorough with the visualization. See the cells and atoms expand with light. Now watch as the light flows around the neck and shoulders, another area that holds a lot of stress. See the light flowing and swirling down the spine and arms, melting away any pain as each vertebra becomes alive with light. The white/ golden light flows down the spine, washing away darkness and pain.

Light flows down the arms into the hands. See the insides of the arms and hands alive with light, even the skin. As your hands and arms glow and your spine becomes alive with the light, bring your attention back to the shoulder blades and the chest area at your heart. As your heart is filled with light from the spiritual sunshine, you become aware of a peaceful, warm glow. An inner smile starts to appear – a feeling of love.

At this point, remember a time that made you feel true, unconditional love; for example, when you saw your favourite pet or a young child running happily and free on a summer afternoon, or a loved one laughing and happy. Cultivate an inner smile, feel the inner smile grow through your entire body. Feel the smile in your skull and brain, eyes, facial muscles, jaw and even your tonsils and tongue. Yes, smile with your brain. Feel the inner smile move anywhere the light swirls.

As the light swirls and flows around the torso, see the internal organs light up with the inner smile. Smile with your lungs, heart, liver, kidneys, oesophagus, even your bladder, your ovaries or prostate. This inner smile is enormously healing. It actually releases endorphins – naturally occurring chemicals that can truly start to heal the physical body. An inner knowing starts to well up within you, a knowing that this light is divine and is leading you home to an abode of peace, your very own connection with the source of all happiness, the breath of life itself, creating your own sacred space.

As you breathe out, see the light emanating outwards in all directions from the cells, pores and atoms – further with every out-breath. *Smile with every cell.* At this point, if you wish, send healing love to those whom you feel need it. If you feel particularly altruistic, send healing love to loved ones, strangers, and enemies. The love vibration will emanate outwards and reach everyone you send it to.

Concentrate, too, on the parts of your own body that need healing; I have healed myself of debilitating illness using these teachings. Truly smiling within your entire body frees any negative, pent-up emotion that can cause disease.

Keep the visualization going as you watch the light swirl and wash around the lower back and hips. Feel the inner smile as the light flows down into the legs and thighs. Feel the smile in those aching knees as, finally, the calf muscles, ankles and feet are full of light and smiling. Feel your entire being alive with light, full of a peaceful, glowing inner smile. *Smile even with your skin.*

The light emanates in all directions, shining through and expanding every atom. Gurus and sages have been telling us for thousands of years that divine consciousness is in everything. Science is starting to confirm that there is, indeed, consciousness in every atom. Use your imagination as a tool to find this divine light within, as the atoms of your body become full and bursting with light, overflowing and expanding with a divine glow. See your entire body dissolve into an inner smile of divine, glowing light.

Visualize light so intense that the atoms of your body feel like they are expanding ever outwards with each out-breath; the atoms so full of light, the space between and within them getting greater and greater until you feel and see your body expanding outwards like golden stardust. The spiritual sunlight has dissolved your physical body into atomic light particles along with your chair, the floor, the walls and the roof of the building you are in.

Visualize the bricks and mortar turn to stardust as the light intensifies these particles, ever expanding outwards. See the street and trees dissolving into stardust.

Expand the visualization outwards as far as possible. You can include any people who have caused you stress; just see them dissolve into light particles and expand outward into space. See all physical phenomena dissolve into light.

See planet Earth; see her alive with vibrating golden particles of light. Believe this is a healing light, healing all living beings on the planet – and the planet herself.

Science tells us that the universe is ever-expanding. Spend time during this meditation just watching the particles expanding further and further away until they have all vanished, until the space has become so vast, as far as your imagination can stretch, until all you perceive is boundless, clear, Blue Sky, empty space – no body, no physical things, just space. See that even the stardust has vanished and dissolved.

As the atomic particles of light and space ever expand outwards, you become aware of a beautiful, warm glow of vast, expansive, clear space where your physical heart would have been before it dissolved into light. Heart feeling and mind feeling become one; your mind has merged with your heart and you can actually feel thoughts calming and sinking down from your head area into your heart area. Move your mind down to your heart and feel your heart and mind merge so that there is no separation, like water poured into water.

The vast, expansive, clear space at your heart at first is like an ocean. Thoughts appear like waves arising out of the ocean and then subsiding once again back into the ocean. Watch the heart-mind until it is so still that it gives the appearance of a calm, tranquil ocean of bliss.

For a while in our meditation, watch the mind and thoughts. Do not hold on to any, or follow them; just watch them like waves arising and then dissolving back into the ocean of stillness as they come and go. When you can hold this feeling of stillness and expand it into an ocean of tranquillity, a feeling of vast, expansive space will appear. You will experience the most extraordinary deep peace and a physical feeling of an inner glow and inner smile just wanting to burst forth. You will find these impossible to contain and they will spill over into your life for others to see.

Dwell within the space between the thoughts, breathing into this space until it expands more and more to reveal boundless, eternal sky-like space. As the appearance of blue sky arises, allow any distant thoughts to disperse like fine wisps of cloud. This eternal, never-changing space at the heart-mind is the source of lasting happiness. This vast, expansive, clear, Blue Sky of stillness *is* the moment; it cannot even be said that it is *in* the moment, because there is no moment in the vastness of it all. *It just is.* How amusing *now* is the petty personal mind, 'poor me'. We can choose to keep the vast, clear, Blue Sky of divine love at the heart-mind, or we can choose the chatterbox, painful heart-mind.

The more space we seek, the more we will find, allowing the heart-mind to become a source of inner peace. An intense stillness will shine from your entire being – no internal noise or chatter, just a serene, empty space of loving kindness at the heart-mind. Divine Mother light can be felt; bringing a feeling of unconditional love for all beings. This is the side effect of stopping all the internal chatter. As a result of this deep inner peace, an inner knowing develops – intuition and deep awareness of an awesome cosmic force of consciousness that is infinitely beyond the petty personal mind and selfish heart. The all-encompassing breath of life itself is revealed. An awareness dawns of the divine feminine, loving and compassionate – the Cosmic Womb from which all life bursts forth. This is perfectly united with a masculine, powerful strength that cannot be broken; whole, timeless, eternal and never-changing, silent, blissful peace – the changing and unchanging in perfect union.

To find and to be in this space is to know. The more you can be the Blue Sky, the more full to the brim of peace your life, and the lives of those around you, will become. When you can truly stop your chattering mind at will, you become flooded with intuition and a divine knowing begins to flow through you. This permeates your life's journey. Doors open, opportunities arise, and you find yourself in the right place at the right time, meeting just the right people you need in your life. Life becomes magical and you become in tune with the infinite.

It really is all Blue Sky: *The vast eternal consciousness of Divine love; when all phenomena are broken down and dispersed, all that can be perceived is a vast space that can be compared to never ending blue sky.* If you search deep within your heart-mind, it is there for you to find and it is not impossible!

Merging your ocean-like heart and sky-like mind as One reveals the clear, expansive, unchanging vastness.

Hold this feeling of an empty, clear, blue sky at your heart-mind for as long as you can.

Become familiar with the thoughts dispersing like clouds. Watch the clear, Blue Sky. Hold it, and take it back with you into your daily life. Become it. Stillness has real strength. Divine love will shine forth!

When you feel ready, imagine all the stardust particles retracting back to you. Feel your physical form once again fixed and solid. Move your fingers and toes whilst saying "I call all my energy back to me." Repeat this three times. Then have a glass of water and a light snack. This will bring your awareness back to here and now.

The First Time Babaji
Appeared to Me

The first time I ever met Babaji was in a dream state. I have had many dreams that have come true in my life and many out-of-body experiences. I have come to know well the difference between an intense, vivid spiritual dream or spiritual experience and a random, mixed-up subconscious dream. Each time I have encountered Babaji, the intense love that I feel could never be replicated in any mundane experience. The detail of every eyelash or line on his face, his beautiful hands and the intense glow that shines from him are indescribable but powerfully clear and more real than waking life itself.

One night, in 2009, I vividly dreamed that I was lost and couldn't find my mother. This dream came at a time when I had finished studying the entire Buddhist Path to Enlightenment and extensive meditation retreats. I was recovering from a debilitating illness that left me bedridden for nearly two years and stopped me in my tracks.

For around twenty-five years I had read discourses from great teachers and listened to their teachings, travelled India and Bali and had come to know various Babas (revered father) but had never come across Haidakhan Babaji or seen a picture of him. The Buddhist emptiness is not a 'void', as some think, but a beautiful, compassionate, blissful space. I had come to discover the emptiness and fullness of it all and had experienced an extremely peaceful state but somehow, something was still missing for me. I felt alone in the vastness. I thought I must be doing something wrong; for me, it felt so impersonal.

When you are about to die, you may, according to your beliefs, grasp at what you hope is a God somewhere out there. Well, I did anyway! So I prayed for the answer . . . which meant I needed someone to pray to! I prayed to whomever or whatever was there to pray to and . . .

. . . the prayer was answered; I had a beautiful visitation. They say that when the student is ready, the guru will appear.

I dreamt that I got on the wrong bus and my mother was on another bus going in the opposite direction. I could see her looking out of the window as it sped off into the distance. I was really anxious to get back to my mother and on the correct bus. Then in slow motion, the driver of my bus turned his head towards me and beamed at me the most unforgettable, most beautiful, compassionate smile. With a loving, melodious voice, he said, "Don't worry; I will get you back to your mother."

I instantly fell in love and awoke with a start. *Wow! Who was that?* I couldn't stop thinking about the bus driver in my dream. I was devastated and elated all at the same time. I know a spiritual experience when I have one! This was one of them. Would I ever see him again? He was unforgettable!

Not too long after that dream, I was in a book shop and saw a picture of him. "That's him! That's him!" I exclaimed as I picked up the book and asked the lady behind the desk who he was, as she had pictures of him above her counter.

"That's Babaji; he is a beautiful being," she replied.

"He appeared to me in a very vivid dream," I told her.

"He makes himself known to people in their dream state when they are ready. He is calling you," she stated with a radiant smile.

I was so excited to hold in my hand a book all about my bus driver and couldn't wait to read it . . . About two or three months after reading the book and internally talking to Babaji all the while, thanking him for appearing to me and asking what the dream meant, I had my first out-of-body visitation from him. By then, I was well into my recovery, using only the Buddhist practices taught to me and applied with blind faith. Buddhism taught me to view the big picture – to see everything as having no solid existence. I saw that the Blue Sky *is* the Mind of the Buddha that we, like everything, dissolve into and I was grateful for that. However, I was at a point where I needed 'God'; a divine presence, whatever you will.

Back to 2009 – *I lifted my head and looked at the clock. It was 3:40 a.m. I could see my body still fast asleep, my head on the pillow. My astral body was wide awake and alert; staring straight into my face was Babaji. He knelt on one knee next to my bed with that familiar, compassionate, divine, loving smile. Beaming at me, he took my hand and gestured at putting a ring on my wedding finger. I saw a pale pink stone, but then it was gone. He said, "Prema magic!" and vanished.*

My physical body awoke with a jolt. I was devastated that he had left and I was bursting with joy and amazement that he has visited me. Then I felt so humbled that I just wept. My next thought was, 'No one will ever believe this.' I was so moved that I literally shook and knew I would never be quite the same again.

The empty vastness I had felt was no longer a void. There really is a loving, compassionate being that knows us and our every thought.

With all the spiritual teaching I had received, I never could have felt such divine love without actually encountering it from Babaji. Afterward, I found out that, within the other belief systems of India, the vastness is looked upon differently – as the Source, the One – and the fountain of pure, absolute love. 'Prema' means divine love and it was certainly utter magic – prema magic!

As cosmic and awesome as the experience was, it left me devastated with the fear that he may not return. You might think I would be grateful for such a blessed visit. With all the teachings on being content with where one is 'in the moment'; not having high expectations or being disappointed and not yearning or craving, you might think that I should be happy. Well, this had certainly taught me I couldn't do it, as all I wanted was for Babaji to be close and to come back!

After hours, days and weeks of sitting in front of his photo and reading everything I could about him, I decided to be content and happily accept that he may not come back. So instead of yearning for his return, I thanked him for showing me how weak my mind is. With this came inner strength and a knowing that he is everywhere – omnipresent. I was also very grateful for that.

In 2010, Babaji returned: *4:42 a.m. – with swirling purple lights and a buzzing sound in my head, I was awake again, my astral body sitting up, my physical body still lying asleep.*

"Baba, you came back; you are here!" I exclaimed as Babaji sat on the edge of my bed.

"Why do you need to go to Glastonbury? I am here with you, not there. No need to go – not tomorrow." He seemed quite stern this time but still had a gentle serenity that shone divine love.

"Oh, come with me, Babaji. Everyone would love you there," I pleaded.

"I am with you," he said and promptly vanished again.

Oh, dear – I was devastated once more that he had left so suddenly, but absolutely ecstatic that he had said "I am with you." I couldn't sleep after that, so I went and sat in front of his picture, thanking him once more. Now I knew that he was everywhere – with me and with anyone who wished to find him.

As it happened, I *was* due to go to Glastonbury the next morning, but it rained so heavily that the trip was cancelled. Babaji knew this, but he also knew that if I went that day, I would not have returned to Glastonbury at a later date and found what he had in store for me.

The next time Babaji appeared to me – in March 2011 – I awoke to find him lying on my bed, staring at me again. He looked very sad; his face turned old and wrinkled before me and a tear ran down his face. "Baba has to go," he said. When he said that, a telepathic message came that Swami, whom I had visited on my travels to India, was going to pass from this life. A 'knowing' also came that both Babas were incarnations of the same divine Shiva; no difference (although both are also thought by some to be an incarnation of Shiva-Shakti).

It was conveyed to me that the divine Father/ Mother shines through the eyes of *all* holy beings. There is only one force – the power of love – and the rays of love shine through the eyes of those who have found the clear, Blue Sky in their hearts and minds.

Swami did die about three weeks later . . . although, in truth, there is no death.

When you have a row of empty glass bottles lined up, they are full of air. When you smash them, the air remains unaffected. The bottles are all occupied by the same air; when the bottles are smashed, the air space remains the same, unaffected.

Holy teachers with clear heart-minds emanate divine love – clear, Blue Sky in all directions, no obstructing thoughts, just a vast ocean of love. This divine, loving space occupies everything.

Kali

As I mentioned at the beginning of this short book, the last thing Babaji told me after throwing the pen and saying, "Write!" was that Kali was on her way. I didn't know what he meant until I finally made my next trip to Glastonbury, early in 2012. In the bookshop next door to where I found the book about Babaji with my bus driver's face, a book stood out vividly as I walked through the door. The cover of the book featured the fearsome face of an elaborately-jewelled black and red goddess with four arms and with her tongue poking out. In large, golden letters, 'KALI' was written across the top. It took my breath away and I knew I had to buy it.

The book was second-hand and the lady said that it had only been brought in that day. Remembering Babaji's words, "Kali is on her way," and that he had told me not to go to Glastonbury the time before, I instantly thought, *'I need to read this book; Babaji wants me to learn about Kali.'* She looked scary, but I knew I needed to get to know her. So, without a second thought, I bought it in the hope that some insight about Babaji's words would be shown to me.

I found out that Kali is an aspect of the Divine Mother. She is very misunderstood, her wrathful image symbolic of slaying our own inner demons – the emotions and feelings we have that make us act in painful ways, such as with anger, jealousy and desire. Desire causes much pain with wanting, yearning, needy, addictive feelings. Anger rises up as our desires are not fulfilled, sending us into a downward spiral of misery until our next temporary fix of happiness.

Kali helps us to overcome our minds, cloudy with the stormy weather of everyday situations.

Kali is a manifestation of the Cosmic Womb, of the mother from which all creation bursts forth and must eventually return. She is time, creation and death – *ever-changing.* When all creation has dissolved, the eternal, never-changing bliss remains. Shiva is the *never-changing.*

Working on one's own mind is no easy task, but it is not impossible and, with steady, gentle practice it is easier than you may think. The key is to realize that you may not get what you want and to be content with that fact.

Find patience in your heart, and allow others their opinions. Give wholeheartedly on every level.

Love all, serve all.

Truth, Simplicity, Love.

∞

∞ ∞ ∞

∞

Kali arrives

4:10 a.m.; *my bedroom door bursts open. The scarves hanging on the back of my door swish back and forth. Very long black and red, bejewelled legs stomp around my bed. A huge, powerful Kali, about ten feet tall, woke me up. I was lying on my side this time, astral body fully alert.*

When in the astral body, one can see in all directions simultaneously; this sounds mad, I know, but anyone who has had an out-of-body experience will know exactly what I mean. Although my physical body was asleep, I could see with my back to the door clearly as my door swung open and the scarves went swinging when Kali tramped into my room. She was so tall that I could only see her legs until she came round in front of me, bent down and poked her tongue out in my face. She telepathically said to me, "Revere Shiva as if you are Kali!"

I was, once more, awake with a start. *Wow! How awesome and cosmic can this possibly get?* I was shaken to the core once again; Kali had just arrived! Babaji said she was on her way, and she was! I felt strong and empowered, yet humbled and tiny. I thought, *'No one will ever believe this.'*

The next day, I couldn't speak and, even now, I hardly speak about it; no words could convey my feelings. I just carry with me a sense of awe and peace. I ponder the words 'Revere Shiva as if you are Kali.' I have Kali to thank for a kind of inner strength that I have found since. She has given me a deep knowing of the power of the divine mother.

In my very limited way, I now understand the words 'Revere Shiva as if you are Kali.' I will try to convey this in words but, as I have said before, words are a very poor means to create or describe a feeling. The feeling is the message, not the words.

No matter what the religion that we either choose or are born into, the teachings are all transmitted by words – holy words, if you like – *The Word*. It seems to me, with my limited mind, that if the true meaning is found in the word or the teachings of any religion, the essence should bring about a common feeling – awe-inspiring, unconditional love at its most human level of understanding – and a realization of omniscience, no separateness, complete *oneness,* a loving, conscious being, the essence of eternal bliss, the source of all that is.

I use the names Shiva and Kali, as these are the characters who have revealed themselves in my personal play to help me arrive at this awesome feeling and understanding. To me, Babaji is Shiva, the male aspect of divinity and Kali the divine feminine, Mother aspect, although there are many aspects.

Babaji is said to be a divine incarnation of Shiva. To me, he has a mind of clear, Blue Sky that shines divinity through his eyes – with no clouds. When I was ill, I needed the reassurance of the divine Mother/Father – and received a vision of Mary, the Madonna, the Mother of Jesus. She looked at me with such compassion that it seemed as if the ocean was in her eyes. Now that I am well, Kali has come. She has given me new strength of character and purpose for whatever is to come in the future.

Kali is a very powerful, compassionate mother aspect of God. She cuts through the minds of illusion, stamping on the demons in the mind, stopping uncomfortable, selfish minds in their tracks. Sometimes Kali allows us to experience our desires until we get our fingers burned and we realize that they may not be as fulfilling as we had expected or hoped, so we start to avoid the things we desired – or, as many find more successful, to let them drop away. She is so kind and loving that she gives us what we ask for – so be careful what you *do* ask for! Just as fire needs wood to burn, eventually the fire consumes the wood itself. In the same ways, the objects of our desires are like the wood – and the fire of desire will eventually burn out.

Kali telepathically said, "Revere Shiva as if you are Kali." She meant that I should look at Shiva with reverence and in awe, intoxicated with pure love, as this is the gateway to divine unity. But at the same time, I knew intuitively that what she meant was to merge the Shiva and Shakti energies. *Wow – tall order! Become Kali and merge as one with Shiva! Blend Shiva/Shakti energies, male/female, father/mother, yin/yang. Become one, like water poured into water. Attain oneness within and without – no dualistic appearance. Non-dual. Divine marriage.*

One night before bed, I asked, "Please, God – please, Babaji – show me who you are without form. Babaji is beautiful and Kali is a fiercely beautiful character in the cosmic play. Please let me know you truly, without form or attribute." As I awoke in the morning, a beautiful, angelic voice said, "It's all Blue Sky." I knew my prayers had been answered. That's when I finally realized what Babaji wanted me to convey. I had come full circle.

Merging the Heart and Mind as One with All That Is

Holding our mind at the heart, which is a vast ocean of bliss, we can find the beautiful spiritual sunlight that evaporates the ocean, every last drop, evaporating it into the light. All physical phenomena, all uncomfortable minds that are drops or waves in the ocean, dissolve into the beautiful, warm sunshine until all that is left is clear, expansive, eternal Blue Sky.

Just as the oceans are gathered up into the sky to make rain clouds and then sent as drops of rain back down to earth to nourish the planet, so the Source gathers us up from the ocean of love and then dissolves us back into the clear, Blue Sky of eternal bliss until it is time to release us, once more, as individual droplets of humanity to start our journeys once again, with free will, to run wild and free as our spirits return to earth. Hopefully, we can help to nourish as many souls as possible. Have confidence that we can come to realize – and *hold* – in our heart-minds a vast amount of clear, Blue Sky. With this, we can make this journey – and our future journeys – as spacious, loving and peaceful as possible for both ourselves and others.

Remember to cultivate an inner smile daily so that it comes naturally, in an instant. Smile with every part of your being; smile even with your skin.

Remember that the clear, Blue Sky permeates every atom within you, your loved ones, your enemies and the entire cosmos. Feel the light beaming from your heart-mind and out through your eyes when you smile. You are a part of the holographic cosmos and your smile is healing and affects every atom in the cosmos. All is *truly* One.

Remember the intention to love all, serve all in service to humanity. It is simple and not impossible! Indeed, it is inevitable – truth, simplicity, love.

Babaji's Approval of This Book

Whilst writing this little book, I kept saying to Babaji, "Well, I hope it's what you want me to write. Please, Baba, you must come back and tell me if it's ok." I would sit in front of his picture, feeling embarrassed that I was even writing a book, all the while knowing that the experiences I have had are out of this world and very unlikely to be believed. Yet, at the same time, thinking Baba must know what he is doing. So with faith and trust, I just kept going, and guess what? He returned! The night of my last page, he came back. How kind! His timing is always perfect, and the joke was on me.

13 February 2013, 2:34 a.m. . . . This time, from being asleep, my consciousness was suddenly in my astral body, floating above my physical body and looking out of a window with no glass. I stood next to Babaji and I was aware of the side of his face and his hair. We were looking out from a white-walled building on what felt like a second-floor balcony. Babaji said, "My favourite view is looking out at the blue sea when it is perfectly still and it meets the clear, blue sky on the horizon. The ocean and the sky merge as one and I wonder, Is the sky reflecting in the sea, or is the sea reflecting in the sky, clear and blue?" Babaji said this with deep contemplation.

We could see amazing, bright blue sea and sky, merging as one at the horizon, with the sunshine sparkling on the sea. I felt that Babaji was the sunshine. I could make out a coconut palm at the side of the white building, too. It was like paradise.

He then vanished. I leaped out of bed to write down the words before I forgot them. I had the realization as he said these words that there is no separation, just a reflection – a merging as one ocean of clear, Blue Sky and bliss. If the ocean heart and sky mind merge and become clear and still, the mind becomes a reflection of divine love.

Then I laughed and laughed. After all I had written, Babaji had shown me the feeling I was trying to convey in this little book with one beautiful, clear picture. The view from that balcony had illustrated exactly what he wanted me to convey. I don't know if I have managed to convey the feeling or not; I will leave that for you to decide. If not, just meditate on the heart as the ocean and the mind as the sky, merging as one reflection of the crystal-clear consciousness of divine love. Hopefully, you will feel the inner smile that a view of paradise brings.

Thank you, thank you with all my heart, Babaji, for your eternal love and kindness. Please bless every heart-mind that reads this, as I dedicate this little book to great enlightenment for all living beings.

Om Namah Shivaya.

Jai Kali.

14 February 2013 – Babaji left his body on Valentine's Day in 1984, so for this little book to be completed on 14 February 2013, without any

conscious effort or planning on my part, I feel is a message of divine love to all his devotees, past, present and future. He is always with all of us, knowing everything in our clear heart-minds, reflecting that same divine love. We just need to remove the clouds.

As a confirmation to me, on the night of 14 February 2013, Swami appeared to me in a dream. He took my hand and kissed it. There is no separation. *It is all Blue Sky.* All is One.

Final Thoughts

It is most important to realize that when the angelic voice said, "It is all Blue Sky," we must not think of this space as 'nothingness'. Within that clear space are many realms of angelic beings and levels of infinite guidance. As Jesus said, "In my Father's house, there are many mansions." (John,14:2) These realms of light-beings are stepping-stones and signposts that may point us forward in our search, but sometimes distract us from the ultimate goal. Always remember that the goal is to immerse oneself in divine love. Clear, Blue Sky in the heart and mind is the gateway to where the ocean of divine love and unity is to be found.

Postscript

How to Find Your Inner Glow: A Meditation with Babaji is an introduction to formal meditation – that is, you sit yourself down somewhere and gather yourself together to perform a routine.

That's where it begins. The really good bit is that, *with practice*, the inner glow, the inner smile, the Blue Sky, the divine love can be recalled in an instant, whether you are meditating, bathing, walking the dog, washing the dishes – it can be with you all the time. Just one tip – sitting cross-legged with your eyes closed is not a good idea when you are driving. This is quite obvious, but any tendency to go too far into an altered state of consciousness whilst driving, operating machinery, walking near a fire, or anything hazardous can lead to accidents. Please use your common sense.

Graham Cailes

Author's Note

Bhole Baba ki Jai! Babaji made himself known to me at a time when I needed him. There is always divine timing at play with divine love.

When the time is right on one's spiritual journey, divine love will never let you down. Trust and faith are powerful links to the divine.

Know with all your heart and soul that your prayers are being heard, even if you feel that they have not been answered. When the time is right and the conditions are in place, the rainbow will appear. That rainbow, the divine plan, will be perfectly and individually tailored for you.

Divine love is kindness itself. Have faith and trust that, if you truly, sincerely search, you will surely find.

As this little book began to draw to a close, I remembered one other dream in which I encountered Babaji; he had prayer beads in his hand and chanted "Om Namah Shivaya" over and over again. This translates, literally, as 'bow down before Shiva' but is often interpreted on the lines of 'take refuge in God.'

On awakening, I knew that he had intended to convey to me to always have the name of God on my tongue and in my heart. I read somewhere that Babaji said that this mantra is more powerful than the atom bomb. It then dawned on me what that meant – for me anyway – breaking through the illusion, the smashing of the bottles and the expanding of the atomic particles until all had dissolved into empty space. When everything is blown apart within the mind, divine love is revealed!

Use the mantra during meditation, once you have found the space, and during your daily life. May divine love bring about peace on earth!

This little book is a tiny introduction to a vast wealth of wisdom that is held by many masters out there. May you find a beautiful teacher on your path to sit with and listen to. When the student is ready, the master will appear. Good luck in your search for truth.

Om Namah Shivaya.

Geri

About the Author

Geri is a born sensitive and natural medium and has been searching for inner peace and truth most of her life. Childhood out-of-body experiences and visions led her forward in that search. A search covering a period of over 25 years, starting with meditation and self-enquiry groups, healing practices and personal study, 12 years with Buddhist teachers, listening to their discourses and receiving personal training in the path to Enlightenment; visits to saints and spiritual masters in India and Bali; studying the principal scriptures in the major religions. Looking for the common thread revealed a deep understanding of the ancient truths.

Then a seriously debilitating head virus stopped Geri in her tracks. This left her with C.F.S and Fibromyalgia.

Geri used what she had learned to help overcome the illness that had left her bedridden for nearly two years and to rise above the physical and psychological trauma.

Then she received the most amazing visitations from Haidakhan Babaji – an incarnation of Divinity which led to the writing of this personal experience.